ARMY OF ONE:

PR & MARKETING FOR THE INDIE FILMMAKER

KEVIN SAMPSON

To Alexandra, Ella, and Kevin, thank you for your love and inspiring me on this journey. I love you!

To the indie filmmaker reading this, the world needs your stories!

CONTENTS

INTRODUCTION

While we may not be physically meeting, I know that the spirit of the person who picks up this book is someone who has a dream, a goal, and wants to better themselves to achieve it. I respect that! I hate books that don't give real answers to the questions I have but instead dance around them. So, I'm trying to brain-dump what I know about PR and Marketing for the underdog, the indie filmmaker, in these pages. Let's get to it with a little introduction.

Who is Kevin Sampson?

I'm a lot of things. I'm a filmmaker, film critic, film festival director, and film publicist. Even though that's quite a few different titles for one person, my journey up to this point is what has given me the unique position to be able to create this book. I earned my MFA in Film and Electronic Media from American University. I spent almost five years as a producer at Arlington Independent Media, a public access station in Arlington, Virginia, which gave me the resources to take Picture Lock (which started out as a film review blog) to a TV show and later radio program. It was there that I became the director of the Rosebud Film Festival in 2013. That gave me the skills and confidence to start the DC Black Film Festival in 2016, in an effort to promote positive images of people of African descent on the big screen. I launched Picture Lock PR in 2017 as a means of representing some of the films I saw, which I'll get into in a bit. I was humbled to receive the 2018 Donald H. McGannon award for my work with women and people of color in media.

I'd simply describe myself as a lover of film and storytelling, with a passion to see all people's stories told on the big screen. However, it's because of my most recent endeavor in founding Picture Lock PR that brings you here.

Why I created this book

After years of being a member of the Broadcast Film Critics Association, Washington DC Area Film Critics Association, the North Carolina Film Critics Association, a Black Reel Awards voter, a juror for film festivals, running two film festivals, and hosting a film review and interview show, I see plenty of films each year. The point is, I know there are great films out there from indie filmmakers that the general public doesn't get to see. I want to try to even the playing field by equipping you, the reader (who I assume is trying to get their film out there), with the necessary tools. I want to help you by using the insight I have, but not in the 'dangle a dream over your head' way like some guru self-help books do. I want you to take away real, actionable steps!

As a lover of film, I've always felt it to be a travesty that some films don't get the love or financial backing that others do. Especially when you have so many duds that hit theaters each year, backed by huge marketing budgets in the Hollywood machine. But, because of my range of experience in the film industry, I've been able to see patterns and loopholes within the business that could make the indie filmmaker more empowered if they know what to look for and what to do.

I launched Picture Lock PR as a way of bridging the gap between hardworking indie filmmakers and the influencers and tastemakers that they can't always reach due to a lack of financial or other resources. I also understand that my PR company may be out of budget for some indie filmmakers. So, I created this book with the hope that the indie filmmaker can have an economical way of getting valuable info on how to generate buzz, get eyeballs on their film, and think strategically about creating a successful outcome for their hard work.

Let's be real. Money and resources can really make a difference. In fact, it will do most of the things I'm going to talk about on a grander scale. But you're probably here because you don't have those funds. I feel you. That's why I made this book for you. I'm so excited to be on this journey with you, because I believe you're reading this because you've got a burning passion, confidence in your craft, and a desire to learn. If you've got the work ethic, like anything else, you can make sure your film is seen by the right people to develop the buzz you need.

Check the tapes; since day one on my show I've always done my best to highlight an indie filmmaker. To wrap this up, I created this book so that indie filmmakers could level the playing field. As an indie filmmaker myself, I know what it's like to grind at a nine to five, shoot and edit a film on the weekends, and hope that you can make an impact in the world with the story you want to tell. I want you to succeed, because the world needs more diverse voices in film. I want you to succeed because the Hollywood system is hard to break into, but you can bring Hollywood to you!

What to Expect

This book will cover what Public Relations and marketing are. It's not an academic deep dive, but we need to cover the basics. I want you to understand how they work together, why they're important, and how to apply them to your film.

Once we've established that, we'll go into setting up your film production from a PR and marketing perspective. We'll cover things like your film's website, press kit, social media, and hacks that you can use to appear as an army. From there, we'll go into the three stages of production and what you should be doing from a PR perspective at each step along the way.

As a director of two film festivals, I'll tell you how to cover the film festival circuit. You absolutely have to establish a goal in hitting the circuit because, while it's a part of the game, it can be costly. You need to know how to not just settle for being accepted, but to take advantage of every opportunity you have to further promote your film during the festival in a way that's genuine and unobtrusive, and I'll teach you how. I've also got some hacks, tips and secrets on how to cut down on festival costs and other areas.

We'll wrap this up with distribution. In this day and time there are so many avenues to, at a minimum, have your film streaming on one of the numerous platforms that will bring you back some sort of return, even if it's pennies on the dollar. Something is better than nothing.

I have included an interview with a filmmaker who has gone down the road of distribution.

This book is meant to speak to every level of indie filmmaker. I hope that it reaches and helps both the amateur and pro in providing valuable information that's scalable to your needs.

THE HARSH TRUTH

The Script Is The Beginning Of Everything.

In my experience, many independent filmmakers fail because of one major mistake: their script sucks. They don't take the time to be vulnerable and have their film vetted by other professionals in the field. That one mistake, turns into a poor film, wondering why their film isn't being accepted into film festivals, and a shelved film in the recesses of their "I once made" shelf. Ouch! I know that may have stung, but if we address this now your film won't be on that shelf but rather the public's streaming playlist or DVD collection.

There are tons of filmmakers in the world. In fact, since 2014 the US has produced 700+ films each year according to Box Office Mojo. That's just the films that get released in America. YouTube sees a billion hours watched every day. Imagine how many films, web series, and documentaries aren't making it to the big screen, or even past your friends and family screening at the house? It's a stiff competition and to make a splash you have to have more than just the will and determination! You could be an amazing director and producer, but everything starts at the script level.

Your script has to be tight, and it needs to be great. Without a great script, you don't have a film worth watching. *The Room* is an anomaly (if you're not familiar with the film, it is arguably one of the worst films ever made, but has an obsessive following). Be willing to have eyes on your script. Get feedback from other filmmakers, writers, and industry mentors.

The truth is, not every film will make it on a major level, so set yourself up to win at the script level so you don't waste time and resources for a dream deferred. Documentary filmmakers, this applies to you too. While many times we go into production on a documentary with one idea in mind and then the film tells us what it's really going to be about, the premise is the same. Your documentary's thesis has to be just as compelling, and certainly the scripted portions you write out have to be as well.

I truly believe that every screenplay that is written from an honest, personal, and passionate place has an audience waiting to see it. The same is true for documentary storytelling. When you write from your heart and shut out thoughts like "Will this make me rich?", "Is this as good as X script?", or "I want to make a twist like that movie", you can win. Money, competitors, and the voice that's self-defeating can't sway you off course. Your only competition is yourself, and your "why" should be to tell the story that you believe the world needs to know. Tap into the creative source that we all feel deep down and write.

Now before you run to IMDb and check out how many scripts I've written, I'm not writing to you as an Oscar-winning screenwriter. Let's be clear on that. I'm writing as a film critic whose seen thousands of films and read tons of screenplays. Remember, I'm on your side; I want you to win!

If your script is a page-turner, or at least has a unique voice, you'll attract others who will want to work with you to see it come to fruition. In fact, you may be a producer who has a script someone else wrote, but it spoke to you in a way that made you want to take on the project. The script and pitch of the film is a huge key to building your village and community around your movie.

If you haven't already done so via film school, books, or workshops, be willing to invest in yourself and learn the craft of screenwriting. You can easily visit the local library and check out a book about screenwriting. I'd definitely suggest finding award winning scripts of films that are in the genre you want to write or of movies you like.

Read and dissect them to understand their structure, and then adapt to your voice. It's like cooking. You can get a recipe that has a base for most people, but you gotta season it to your own taste!

So, why am I spending time talking about how things need to be great at the script level? It's extremely important in working to separate yours from the rest of the pack. Many times in the indie film world, we forget that this is a film business, because our passion puts blinders on certain things that are glaringly obvious to others. We write what's popular rather than what we know. Here's the secret, the more personally you write, the more universal it will be. In other words, more people than you think can relate to the bullying you endured while you were in high school and will see themselves in your characters and story.

It has been said there are seven basic plots in the world of storytelling: overcoming the monster, rags to riches, the quest, voyage and return, comedy, tragedy and rebirth. Universal storytelling is the best form of storytelling because it connects and resonates. You can achieve that with your audience when you write what you know. People will respond because they know your story personally or they see a genuine story they've never experienced before.

Be willing to screen your film and get eyes on it early.

As a critic, we screen major motion pictures before they're released. As soon as we exit the theater we're asked, "What did you think?" by publicists. When I go to film festivals as press, I don't pay to see a film, but you better believe the publicists of the film ask for my coverage or thoughts on the film after I've seen it.

Once you've shot your film, be willing to screen it before it hits the festival circuit or before you try to seek distribution. We all know there are three different films: the one you write, the one you film, and the one you edit. Feedback from an audience is crucial in making sure that a diverse group of people will watch and understand your film. The big studios do it all the time for a reason. We spent plenty of time talking about how the script has to be great, and sometimes what is written on the page may not make it once the film hits the production stage. The shift, for whatever reason, that a film makes in coming out as the final edit versus the original script has to be checked. If jokes didn't hit, or edits were too abrupt, or scenes need to be cut down, etc. you still have a chance to make changes before your major push. This is a crucial point in the business process of filmmaking that many indie filmmakers miss!

Set yourself up to win and make plans to have a screening before you hit the circuit. It could be your premiere, but make sure you have a way of capturing audience feedback. Don't limit yourself to your friends' thoughts, but try to rope in people you don't know. If you can get a critic to come and give feedback, that's a plus. Seek honest feedback, not just a pat on the back. Yes, you do deserve a pat on the back because you made a film. That's not something everyone can say! However, if you want the film to go past your network of friends and family, seek honest feedback.

If you're willing to get eyes on your script before you go into production, and screen your film once it's complete, this book is for you! It's going to take that kind of humility and understanding of the business of cinema to make sure your film makes a splash. If you're down, let's get started.

CHAPTER 1
THE LONG GAME

What is Public Relations?

The Public Relations Society of America defines Public Relations (PR) as a strategic communication process that builds mutually beneficial relationships between organizations and their publics (or core audiences). For our purposes, PR is simply building intentional relationships between your film and the main audience who will watch it. One of the key words in that definition above is strategic. The word strategy is packed with nutrients. It means that thought, wisdom and energy came together to form a plan that would be executed. PR is about not spinning your wheels or throwing ideas at a wall to see what sticks. It's about digging into Google Analytics, other data sources, and planning how to reach the people who would be the most interested in your film.

The American Marketing Association defines marketing as the activity, set of institutions, and processes for creating, communicating, delivering, and exchanging offerings that have value for customers, clients, partners, and society at large. Which basically means all the efforts you put into making people aware of your film, getting them interested in it, knowing how to find it, etc. Marketing is certainly a process. The good thing is, it can be learned.

Good public relations and publicity are equally as important as effective marketing and advertising strategies. In fact, they work best when they are done conjointly. This dynamic duo is what will help your indie film stand out. They will ensure that at the very least, your film will be viewed with respect for the effort you put in to building something around it.

How PR and Marketing work together.

If PR is strategic relationship building and marketing is the process of creating, communicating, delivering and exchanging offerings that have value, then the combination is simply planning out how to best reach your audience, executing and following through. While their strategies may differ at times, the goals should be the same. Without results-focused objectives that match your goals, PR often produces content without real purpose.

How PR firms work for films.

Large PR firms have a lot of advantages. They save you a lot of time and legwork in creating a buzz around your film. You want to get critics to see your film? You want to get interviewed by press? You want coaching on how to talk in an interview? PR firms can do all of that and more for you because they have the knowledge, experience, and relationships. They are the trusted gatekeepers and middlemen/women to studios and critics.

Aside from being a bridge, PR firms also have the experience in creating messaging to the public, critics, and film festivals that grab their attention. So you're paying to ensure that you get your desired results. While no firm will give you a guarantee, they will work hard for you and aim to please. They save you the headache of doing the legwork.

Here's a secret. Some films sell themselves, some films can be sold, and some films are a struggle to sell for PR firms. Why do I mention that? Even the big firms can have issues promoting a film at times. The latest Marvel Cinematic Universe film is always going to sell itself while indie films may have to be sold to an audience. So it's not just about getting people's attention, but it's also about converting that attention into a desire to see a film. Frankly, sometimes people just aren't interested in seeing a certain film. I've seen screening giveaways from publicists that barely had bodies present. My point is, if third-party PR firms have to figure out how to gain traction to convert awareness of an upcoming film into a desire to see the film, so can you.

How to apply it to your film.

Well that's what we're going to cover through the course of this book. Creating your own PR and marketing will take a lot of sweat equity, but hey, you're planning on shooting (or have shot) a film! That's a task in itself. You're used to putting in work. The key is to lump PR and marketing into your pre-production so it won't be a task.

Now that we're on the same page in regard to what PR and marketing is and what that means for your great film, let's get into the nuts and bolts of what you should be thinking about in pre-production.

Reel Thought: *If you ever do get a PR firm to help you with your film, make sure they get and understand your film. You don't want to hire someone that is doing it just for the check. Make sure that the firm is passionate about your film. I don't take on clients if I don't feel passionate about their film. That might be a personal thing, but I want to be excited about spreading the word and you should get that kind of treatment as well!*

CHAPTER 2
SETTING UP YOUR WEBSITE/EPK

I f you aren't thinking about creating a website for your film, that needs to change right now. You might say, "But Kevin, I don't know how to build a website!" No excuses. There are plenty of sites that will do all the coding work for you if you drag and drop your messaging, media, etc. into their interface.

Websites are a must-have for any filmmaker these days, but especially indie filmmakers. They signify a certain level of investment in the film. It gives the film credibility in that the filmmaker took the time to create a central information hub for anyone to learn more about it. It separates the people that say they have a film out (which may be true), from the people that not only have a film out, but understand how to build community around it.

Your site also allows you to capture e-mails from people that visit the site. It will allow you to tell people where they can see the film playing next. It will allow you to have a trailer embedded in it so that potential reviewers can get a taste of the film and decide if they want a screener. It will allow you to show critics and studios all of the press and awards you've accumulated while the film has been on the festival circuit. And guess what! You didn't even have to talk about the film yourself. The information is there for public consumption. Most importantly, a website surrounding your film is an undeniable sign that your film exists and that you take it seriously.

For anyone with a short film who is rolling their eyes right now, there are plenty of one-pager websites like strikingly that you can use to create a site. Again, this is scalable to your understanding of what you want to do with your film and budget, but keep in mind that a first impression speaks volumes. Having a Facebook page isn't enough to stand out from the crowd, because everyone has a Facebook page for their film.

Electronic Press Kit Tutorial for Film

An Electronic Press Kit (EPK) is your press kit in an electronic form. In the past, it's been predominately done as a downloadable document (PDF) that you can easily send to festivals and press. These days, it's easy to cover everything via your website. The right EPK can get your work seen by critic, get your film accepted into festivals, boost your crowdfunding and more. There are plenty of formats and intricacy levels to EPKs that you may find with a simple Google search. I'm going to tell you from a film critic and festival director's perspective what we like to see in your EPK.

The Basics

Even though it's called a press kit, remember that you're planning to send it to more than just press. We're thinking long game from concept to post-production, so if you set it up in pre-production, your movie's website can be a powerful marketing tool. It can help you with fundraising as well as pitching your film to possible collaborators. You can even keep a running blog on the progress of the film to invite your community to take the journey with you.

Remember, if your idea is in your head, no one else knows what it looks like. An EPK in the pre-visualization stage can really make your film come to life. Certainly, an EPK based off of the actual production will work wonders in the post-production phase of your film.

Whatever you do, be sure your EPK supports and informs your film. Paul Bruce, Director of Edinburgh Short Film Festival said it best, "A bad EPK tells you almost nothing about the film and everything about the people involved in making it." Your EPK should be unique, clear, and it should compel the viewer to want to see or learn more about your film. The key is that it should be in service of the film itself, not you. Think of your EPK not just as a means to get attention, but as a way to build your community around the film.

What's the Hook?

What's the draw that will get people interested in seeing the film? What would interest a critic in reviewing the film? Well, first we have to make sure people know about it, and this is where having a good elevator pitch that's base-level easy to understand is important. Before you purchase a meal at a restaurant, you prefer to see a beautiful image and mouth-watering description of it, get a recommendation from your waiter or from hundreds of reviews on Yelp, right? The same rules apply to your film. You have to have the initial draw, and then the following will help reel people in further.

They don't say, "Keep It Simple, Stupid" for nothing. When you're marketing your film, simplicity is key. Create a strong theme or hook that you will use for your film. The question to ask is: what's going to make your production unique? Is it based on an unbelievable but true story? Is it a 'be careful what you wish for' story? Is it guaranteed to have people check under the bed before they go to sleep? Find your hook and build your EPK around it.

If you struggle with creating a simple hook, do your research! Don't forget the seven basic plots I mentioned earlier (again they are: overcoming the monster; rags to riches; the quest; voyage and return; comedy; tragedy; and rebirth.) Whatever your film is about, it likely fits into those seven themes and more likely than not, there is a film out there that is similar to yours. Look for similarly themed films that market themselves well in order for you to get inspiration and gain knowledge. Then, create your own masterpiece for your film.

You might ask yourself: why am I asking you to find the hook or angle that separates your film from the rest? Because that's what PR firms do. We look for the hooks that the consumer will latch on to.

EPK – Basic Requirements

Let's dig in to what your web EPK should consist of and look like. EPK requirements vary by outlet. However, when it comes to a festival or distributor requesting it, or if you're in the initial phase of constructing it, it usually includes these basics:

1. Website

2. Teaser/Trailer

3. Film poster/stills

4. Logline & Synopsis

5. One Sheet

6. News/Press Information

7. Cast & crew bios

8. Contact details

Keep in mind that your PDF version would have the same parts, minus the teaser/trailer. So do the work once, but use the same information for both your web EPK and your PDF document.

Creating Your EPK

Let's get into the nuts and bolts of what your EPK should look like. For the purpose of keeping up with the following information, I view the EPK as your website, while an actual Press Kit should be located on the site as a downloadable pdf. The reason I distinguish between the two like this is because the website should virtually have all the information that your press kit has and more, with the ability to play video. It's a lot like going to view a house (your website) and then walking away with the brochure (the downloadable pdf). The brochure has all the succinct takeaway information you need on the house you just saw, but walking through it is the real experience.

1) Website

For anything these days, if it's supposed to be worthy of attention, it likely has a website at the very minimum. Your film is no different. You have to have a website for your film because it says, "This film is worthy of it's own domain name and someone is working to make sure it's seen". While a Facebook page is essential, it still doesn't have the same impact that a dedicated website does. The social media pages and handles are a part of your publicity and community building, which we'll get into later, but the website is the flag on the moon symbolizing that your film exists and it is here to stay.

As a film critic, I have more interest in checking out an indie film if it has its own site than if it does not. As the producer and host of Picture Lock, I find myself frustrated if my guest doesn't have a place where I can find information as I do research for their interview. The absence of a web home automatically puts thoughts in my head about the filmmaker's level of seriousness, even on the indie film level.

> Reel Thought: *Creating a website is something to seriously think about as you make your film and seek press attention. However, let's say you can't afford a cheap website. Do you have your IMDb page up and complete? How can a potential interviewer find out all the info they need online or will you provide them with all that information? The website will get it done for you. It's worth budgeting for in your pre-production process.*

In designing your website, there are a few "must have" items that are essential. You should always have a trailer or at least a teaser for your film. A critic may not have time to view your full film, but if they have a couple of minutes they may settle in to view your trailer. Your film's poster and stills from the film and behind the scenes (bts) should be available for viewing as well. Your film's logline and synopsis also need to be included on the site to give insight into what the film is about. A one-sheet can also be available for download as a pdf somewhere on the site. Your main cast and crew bios and headshots (particularly with actors) should be on display on the site. Contact information as to how immediately send you a message through the site or via e-mail should visible. Your social media pages and/or handles should be posted as well.

Let's dive further into these pieces of your website. I want to make sure you know how to construct them so that it's attractive and matches the expectation of what I've come to expect to see as a critic and publicist.

2) The Trailer/Teaser

You should always have a trailer or at least a teaser for your film. A trailer is a fleshed out promotion of a film that gives the audience the gist of what they can expect to see in the film. A teaser is a short promotional video that alludes to what you will see in the film or what the film may be about, but it is meant to get the audience interested in seeing more. Again, a critic may not have time to view your full film, but I'll give you a couple of minutes if I'm intrigued by the film's concept or images. Make sure the trailer/teaser does the following:

1. Gives an accurate glimpse of what the viewer can expect to see.

This is your opportunity to show the film's tone, plot, cast, and pace. Be sure that the viewer can give a basic plot synopsis after seeing the trailer. Whatever the tone

(I'll call it vibe) of the film is, let it be seen in the trailer. It's like an appetizer before eating the main course. Be sure to show the main characters in your cast and balance their screen time in the trailer with the amount of screen time they have in the film. By that I mean, if you scored Denzel Washington in the film and he's only in the movie for a few scenes, don't feature him the entire time in the trailer! It's an awesome win, but gives a false sense of the movie. This may seem like a no-brainer, but I've seen this happen before. Again, tailor this information for your film. If there's a twist in the film and a character needs to look like they're involved but dies for example, create the trailer so that when the viewer sees the film they're surprised.

2. Don't try to put every "cinematic" shot or moment into the trailer.

Some filmmakers make the serious mistake of putting an overabundance of what they think are compelling moments or shots in their trailer in an effort to make their film seem more epic or gripping in tone. If you're doing that in exchange of giving us a clear understanding of what your film is about, you may be covering up the fact that your film is not that great. I hope that didn't seem too harsh, but honestly, that's what we think as critics. We want to see some cool shots of Viola Davis spitting during a passionate speech, but too much of that is a turn off.

3. Don't give everything away.

Have you ever watched a comedy and the best lines were in the trailer? What's the point of watching the film? If the best moments are in the trailer, you may have a problem. Save something for your viewer to be shocked by or crack up at when viewing the full length film. Whatever genre of film you have, don't tell the entire story and give away all of the best moments in the trailer.

4. It shouldn't be very long.

I've had "trailers" sent to me that were three plus minutes in length. The Motion Picture Association of America (MPAA) requires trailers to be two and a half minutes max! If you can't tell the story in two and a half minutes, you're doing something wrong. You're a filmmaker, aka a storyteller! Tell the story quickly and efficiently, but also effectively.

This is also a place to make sure you get fresh eyes on the progress of your work. If you're having trouble cutting together a good trailer, perhaps you shouldn't be cutting it. If you're serving as the editor on your film as well, try letting someone else put the trailer together. I guarantee they'll cut it in a way that you hadn't thought of or seen. Don't make the mistake of doing it yourself if you can't be objective and if you feel you have to get a certain shot in! The trailer should be focused on the other things I've listed, so if you can't get it there, do the film a service by giving it to someone else to cut together or have the humility to get good feedback and apply it.

3) Film Poster

They say a picture's worth a thousand words. That's why every film deserves a good poster. A poster can tell a story in itself. The right poster does everything that a trailer does except it has one bonus: It draws upon the viewer's imagination in a way that the trailer can't. Great posters are a work of art. Your eyes take in the full image and then dissect everything in it. What are the cast and individual character's faces saying? Are there people in it at all? What is the typography emoting?

Conduct a quick google search for the best movie posters of all time and you'll see exactly what I mean. They're absolute works of art that speak to you. In short, the poster should make you interested in seeing the movie, and should be remarkable (worthy of conversation) in it's own right.

If you're not a graphic artist, seek one out. There are plenty of online collaborative platforms where businesses can seek out freelancers to do work for economical prices. I've listed them in the resources section of this book. Make sure that you budget to hire a great graphic artist. The awesome thing about hiring one of these professionals online is that you can sift through portfolios until you land on the ones that you feel have the work history and the vibe that you want.

4) The Logline & Synopsis

A logline is a one (let's strive for one but it could occasionally be two) sentence description that condenses the main theme and/or conflict of the story. For those of us of a certain age, do you remember the TV Guide? (Everyone else, Google it.) They had the best loglines. There wasn't enough space on the page or screen to have more than one sentence about what the scheduled film or tv show was about. Think TV Guide when you're creating your logline. How can a reader understand the film in one sentence?

Loglines are sometimes used on posters, so you may want to look at movie posters for inspiration here as well.

Come up with a few different loglines then ask for feedback from people you know. If they can walk away with a good understanding of what your film is about, you're on the right path.

Now, on to the synopsis. I like to think of the synopsis as your elevator pitch written out in a few paragraphs. It's longer than the logline, but is still a brief, concise summary of what your film is about. The synopsis should not be a plot summary that tells the beats of your movie. Instead it should give the reader information on the main characters and the arch of the story.

Reel Thought: *Plan on writing a brief synopsis, synopsis, and long synopsis. The brief synopsis will be a quick hit for your one-sheet. The synopsis is the main one you'll use. The long synopsis can be a little more in depth and would likely be passed along to potential reviewers.*

Working out the film's synopsis can also be helpful in pre-production as you develop your idea for the screenplay. It can be your guiding force in pre-production and then once you're in post-production you can tweak it where necessary so that it represents the final film.

5) One-Sheet

A one-sheet is something that seems to be fading away these days because of the use of the internet on an indie level. However, it's something that you always want to have because it's better to have and not need than need and not have. The reason a one-sheet is good to have is because it is a single sheet of paper that can be handed off to someone that has all the information they need to know about your film. Think of it as an in-between for your business card and EPK. A good one-sheet has a strong visual image on one side and information about the film on the other. Here's some of the info that you want to include:

Contact information. I'm putting this at the top of the list because it's like taking a test when you were in elementary school and forgetting to write your name at the top. You can be so busy focused on the bigger things, that you forget the simple, sure shots. Be sure to include your name, role, address, phone number, email address and website. If your document is double-sided, be sure to put this information on both sides so it can be found easily.

Title. Again, this is a no brainer, but you want to make sure the title of your film is portrayed clearly.

Logline and Genre. We just covered the logline in the previous section, so we're clear on that. By adding the genre, this allows whoever is checking out the one-sheet to quickly know specifically the type of film you're presenting. If the image on the front is of a scary looking zombie with the title "Living Amongst the Living Dead", it would be easy to assume that it's a horror film. However, if it's a documentary about horror makeup and the artists who create it, that's a totally different film. We're seeking clarity in what the project is about and that will help to give it, because you don't want to mislead your audience.

Brief synopsis of the project. You have a limited amount of space on the paper that you can use, so that will limit the amount of words you use. Make them count by having a tight synopsis that says everything a reader needs to know about the film, but do it without being verbose.

If you don't do your own graphics, keep visuals, such as photos or still images, in mind to convey to a graphic artist. The visuals should strive to communicate the tone, theme, setting, and premise of your concept in a single image, if possible. Remember, a picture paints a thousand words.

6) Cast & Crew Bios

It's very important to have your cast and crew bio on the site. The cast members are the faces of your film. There are plenty of times that I've seen the trailer of a film and recognized a face in the cast from a prior film I've seen. I love playing the, "What movie was it that I saw them in?" game.

A good idea is to put a link to their IMDb page. That way, whoever is viewing the site can quickly find your cast/crew members' past work. I find this extremely helpful when I'm crafting the review of a film. If your film is not well-known, but your actor is, I can quickly jog my audience's memory by including the movie title that they may have seen said actor in. I can also vouch for the actor by saying "I saw him/her in X and they were equally wonderful". If they're unknown, it also gives credibility to at least list that they've been in other films. The same goes for listing your above the line crew. These are the little touches that you may not generally think of, but from a critic's perspective can be really helpful for us. And if you help us, we can help your film.

You may be a little worried if your cast and crew is not well known as an independent filmmaker. Don't. Everyone has to start somewhere. Just like interest in a bank, over time, your cast and crew's resume will grow and will be larger. However, perhaps a good substitute for your cinematographer's link would be their demo reel if it's very strong. The same could go for your actors.

Depending on how much space you have on your site's page, it may be good to link any social media handles as well. As a critic, I like to tag filmmakers, their film's handle, and, if I can, add in members of the cast or crew to tag. I want my review to be read just as you want it to be written. So if I'm highlighting a performance or the cinematography in a film, it's really helpful if I don't have to search for the social handles. No matter where you are in your filmmaking experience, be sure to have your cast and above the line crew featured on the site with additional links to find out more information on them.

7) News/Press

Be sure to create a running blog on the site of news about your film and any press the film has received. You want to document the journey of your film and this is where you can do it. By creating a running, living narrative behind your film it will allow you to tell a story about your film.

Intentionally crafting a story is really important, because while laurels may prove that your film has been accepted into a festival or won an award, that's all they do. How was the film received at the festival? Did the whole cast and crew hit the red carpet? Was there a viewer who came up to you emotionally moved after the screening who gave you a memorable thought about the film? This is where you can show and tell those moments with images and words.

Additionally, if you went on a local morning show to talk about your film or had a write up in the paper you should post that! There have been plenty of times in doing my research for having a filmmaker on my radio show, that I've looked at an interview that he/she has done prior to mine. It helps better inform me of the film, and helps in crafting questions and even getting a vibe for the person I'm going to interview. As a festival director, I'm always happy to combine promoting a film by using a recent interview that's already been done on the film. Most importantly it builds your film's credibility and story for anyone who checks out the site. Plus, when you finally get to come up for air and look at what you've done with your film, you can be a proud mommy or daddy with the collection of clips and articles reminding you of the journey from start to finish.

8) Contact Details

You created the film and your site to be seen! This is where you can start to build your community. There are a few things to do.

Make sure you list your contact information on the site, and/or have a contact form for the user to fill out. This should be separate from your social media buttons. You run the risk of losing someone who wants to get in touch with you if you force them to contact you through social media. So whether you have a general inquiry e-mail or use a form, make sure that someone can reach out directly without hurdles.

On the flip side, you should catch visitors' e-mail as they come through the site. There are multiple ways to achieve this. It could be done with a pop-up that can be implemented upon initial entry or through a sign-up form embedded in the site. At the least, you should have some sort of way to create a list of fans of your work. This list is not only key for your current film, but for projects in the future. More than likely, if someone likes one of your projects, they won't mind hearing about and seeing your future works.

Last but certainly not least, you have to have your social media visible on the site. Whether it's simply a logo that people can click on or a side bar that shows the latest tweets from your film, your social media presence is a must. It's certainly a great way to have people follow the film and join the conversation.

CHAPTER 3
PRE-PRODUCTION

Creating a marketing plan

If you're like me, when it comes to creating art, I really don't want to plan it, I just want to do it. Planning takes away some of the creativity. Planning takes away time that you could be working on said art. Planning takes brain power to create strategies, timelines, and the like. And yet, planning is absolutely essential if you want to make some noise!

Since we know we'll have to suck it up and come up with a marketing plan if we want to be really successful, we might as well just do it. Doesn't it make sense to do it all in your film's pre-production period? You're already in planning mode. While most filmmakers and producers are thinking about the schedule breakdown, you're not the average filmmaker. You're thinking about the film business. The business of film requires that you have a strategic plan that will start from the moment you step on set to the moment you step on stage to receive an award and all the way until you eventually hang the film up. Notice, I didn't say move on to the next film. You may still be working the PR and marketing plan for your completed film while in production for the next one.

I won't get into a long, drawn out nuts and bolts of "how to write your marketing plan" chat. You can certainly Google how to create one. Instead, I'd rather tell you a few of the things that you should keep in mind, and you can build from there. Remember, everything is scalable to fit the need of your film.

These days the best film marketing all contain some style of what I like to call Drip Drop Marketing. (There are tons of terms for this, but it's the one I like.) The big studios understand how to slowly let out information and media about their film, consistently remind you the film is coming, flooding you with marketing leading up to and through the film's run in the theaters, and then repeating it when the DVD comes out.

This can be applied to the indie filmmaker's release as well. You may not have a nationwide release, but if you have a video on demand (VOD) or streaming release, you can use the same model. Even on the film festival circuit the concept can be applied.

First Things First

In the pre-production stage you should be focused on making the public aware of your film by building interest and community. Setting up your film's website and social media pages are low hanging fruits that will allow you to start that. So knowing where you are going with your film in post-production is the biggest thing you want to figure out in the pre-pro stage because it will inform your marketing efforts. Your marketing efforts can certainly affect your budget and you need to make sure that you include PR and marketing in your budget. For example, you can create pages and handles on social media for free and try to get authentic shares amongst friends or fans of your film. However, if you really want to cut into undiscovered audiences you should set aside money for paid promotional ads.

My biggest ask is that you start engaging the public early! It's going to take a while before your film is in a stage where it can be viewed by an audience. If you play your cards right, you will have snowballed the development of a community over the course of time rather than scrambling to gain one at the last hour.

Your Social Media

I always suggest that my clients are on at least the big three: Facebook, Instagram, and Twitter. There are so many different social media platforms and apps that it would be difficult to keep up with everything. Know your film and which platforms may work for you outside of the big three I believe are a minimum. For instance, if you're doing a documentary on quilt making then you may want to add a Pinterest page to engage a potential audience with ideas for patterns, examples of a quilt from one of the subjects in the film, etc. If you're making a film about teens finding themselves in high school, you should definitely be on Snapchat.

Why those three? Facebook has over two billion users, Instagram has one billion, and Twitter has over 330 million. Outside of numbers and some of the obvious capabilities that each platform gives, they are also very common widgets. So when you create your website on Squarespace or WordPress, or create your mailing list in Mailchimp or Constant Contact, you can easily plug those share buttons into those platforms.

When you're settled on your film's title, grab up all the social media handles at one time. Cross check the various platforms to make sure that you can use the same handle across all the social you use with your film. It makes things simple for all involved when you can say "follow @prthemovie on all social media" versus "we're @prthemovie on Twitter, @prthefilm on Instagram, and prmovie on Facebook". I'm checking out the second you say I have to memorize more than one handle. If you have to adjust because you can't keep things synchronous across platforms, do what you have to, but if you're planning this early you should be able to come up with the right handles.

Be sure to come up with the proper hashtags for your film in pre-production as well. That way, from the start, you can have the running history of your film tied to the hashtags of your film. Also, viewers, fans, critics, and more can join the conversation by searching for your hashtag. At the minimum have the film's title and create unique, memorable, but poignant hashtags from there.

Being Efficient on Social Sites

As I talked about before, make sure you have your social links on your website. As an army of one, you have to work smarter within your social media game. Having automated posts can save you tons of time. There are sites like Buffer, Tweetdeck, and Hootsuite that can allow you to manage your various social media by monitoring, scheduling posts, and connecting various outlets. I want to bring your attention to one that has been invaluable to me: If This Then That.

If This Then That (IFTTT) is an easy way to get your apps and devices working together, and it's totally free. IFTTT allows you to post to multiple platforms at once.

It also allows you to schedule posts that will automatically go out when you want them to, whether it's once a week, daily, etc. through a simple chain of statements called applets.

Here's an example of how it's a time saver. Say you make a status update on your film's Facebook page that you also want to go out to Twitter. You can make an applet that says, "If you post a status update on Facebook, then publish a tweet on Twitter also." By linking up your various social platforms via a few applets, you cut down your social media posting time. As soon as you make an Instagram post, you know that it will post on your Facebook page and Twitter stream as well.

I've never been the biggest social media guru. I've always felt like social media's need for consistency

> Reel Thought: *Think of IFTTT as a way to consistently post an evergreen message. Ex. Telling people to check out your film's trailer. You'll still have to do content creation, but it helps you with evergreen content and dissemination of one post to multiple platforms.*

can be tedious when balancing home life, work life, and more. I would always forget to tell folks to tune in to Picture Lock at 3PM on Fridays, but with IFTTT I created an applet that would do it for me. Now, every Friday and Monday when the show airs, whether people tune in or not, I have a post as a reminder. IFTTT is a life hack that will help you be an army of one!

Document your production from the beginning

Pre-production is King. We know this in film, and it's the same in PR and marketing for your film. If you prepare and plan for PR and marketing to be part of your workflow during the pre-production process, it won't sneak up on you later.

Plan for the documentation of your project throughout the production and post-production process. Who will take photos, behind the scenes (bts) footage, and how will they get to social media? Should you and your producer have access to the Instagram account to cut down on your responsibilities? Do you have money in the budget for a social media handler?

With your social media hashtags ready to go as we talked about earlier, you can build a buzz around the film and make sure your cast and crew knows what to use when making posts. This is all apart of community building. Imagine how much confidence will be instilled in your cast and crew receiving the "plan" from you with your social media push and outreach. It shows that you've put thought into all the aspects of your filmmaking and that you plan on this film being a success. That's something anyone can get behind, especially when they already signed on to participate in the film because they believe in it in the first place!

Another thing to think about is who you may reach out to with regards to press and media about your film. If you're doing a local film, it might be smart to let the local paper or biggest local online outlet know that you are about to begin production on a home grown film. That way your community can get behind the film ahead of time.

Draft a list of critics that may check out your film or have you on their podcast. Are there film podcasts out there looking for indie filmmakers to come on their show? Find out, and have e-mail copy drafted and ready for when you release or are about to release the film.

This list building process will help you not only for this film, but for future films as well. Remember, one of the big differences between you and a PR firm is their contacts. By gathering and organizing contacts you can get surgical with your film's marketing. You can start to group together critics by location, podcasts, by ease of accessibility (who you can quickly get in touch with versus who it may take time to get on their schedule), or television news producers by whatever category you want to put them in.

> Reel Thought: *Organize your list of press and media by category and region. This will come in handy when you have a premiere in Washington, D.C. and want to know who to invite in the DMV (depending on where you're from that's DC, Maryland, Virginia area not where you get your license). The more specific you are in your organization the better you can tailor-make your engagement with the public. Know the audience you want to reach with your film, and know how to contact that audience for outreach efforts.*

Final Thoughts

I can't help but repeat that this is all scalable, but make sure you know your film existed. If you don't, the world won't. What I mean by that is by documenting your film's production via photo and video, creating a paper trail of articles written on the film, and seeking video spots, much like b-roll, you'll have visual evidence to supplement your film's existence. Capturing all of that starts in the pre-production process by creating a plan to do it.

Generating media buzz around your film is what will help you to win attention from the public and from critics. There are plenty of times that I have been intrigued to find out more about a film and watch it due to the reminder of it from seeing or hearing about it through various outlets. Try to get on everything you can, while being strategic about the audience you want to reach.

Ultimately, the best form of marketing is word of mouth. How many times do you go to a restaurant and ask the waiter/waitress "what's popular?" Hopefully, you're creating a film that will generate that kind of excitement, but by doing these things you are definitely laying the groundwork for an optimal PR and marketing campaign.

Remember that you're not alone in the process. Everyone who is helping make the film is a marketer. Make asks of your cast and crew. By having the hashtags and social media handles ready to go, you can get them joining in on the community building. If your DP is taking a photo of a production meeting and posting to his or her Instagram page, that helps your cause. You can't force anyone to participate, but hopefully you build a team that will gladly do it.

CHAPTER 4
PRODUCTION

You're in it and there's no turning back now! You have a cast and crew signed up to work together with you to create your film. You have dates on the calendar and locations reserved. You probably have the regular doubts that come with executing a huge project and may have the urge to throw up from this overwhelming sense of "this is really happening!". It is, and you can do it!

Now that we've acknowledged those facts, it's time to crush it! A pearl of wisdom that Victoria Negri told me in regard to directing Robert Vaughn (in what would be his last film) at the age of 27 is, "I had to say to myself, he said yes for a reason. He wants to be apart of this. This is my chance to act with a legend. So you've gotta just do it!" Everyone involved has signed on to do the project because they believe in you and the story you're trying to tell. Let that sit with you for a moment. Go ahead. I'll wait for you on the next paragraph.

This isn't a film production book. So I'm sure that you know what to do in regard to creating the film. This is all about the PR and marketing surrounding it. It's easy to get laser focused on filming your production and miss capturing moments. So be sure to have your "PR and marketing documentarians" in place.

In addition to the team of people you have ready to work with you, you also have all of the pre-production work and documents that you put together to guide you. That's another boost of confidence! It's time to execute what you've already outlined in pre-pro so this chapter won't be long.

Reel Thought: *Invite your local press to set one day. What better way to establish a relationship than that? Lunch is on you, and the experience is something different for them. It never hurts to ask, and you just might get a cool story out of it!*

Remember to delegate. Filmmaking is not a solo sport. You can't do it all, but if your pre-production is on point, you will have mini you's on the team so you can relax and focus on creating your cinematic masterpiece. So relax and let go. You can pick the rucksack back up in post.

CHAPTER 5
POST-PRODUCTION

Congratulations! You've got the film in the can! You did it! Hats off to you. So many people say they are filmmakers, but you're actually doing it. Whether this is your first film or you've been around the block a few times, you did it! So pop that bottle, have that wrap party, and then come back when you're ready to get back to work!

Now that you've celebrated wrapping on the film. It's time to really start working. I want to get you thinking about something as you engage in the technical side of the post-production process. This will help you not have to double back as you work.

As You Edit

While you're editing and seeing the film come together, start looking for clips that would be good for your trailer and good to send to press. In fact, create a folder and start dropping the best stills as well as 15, 30, and 60 second scenes. I don't want you to go overboard in doing this, but it will save you time when you start looking to get press involved. It will also save you time when dealing with film festivals if you have your stills and clips ready for them.

Remember that the clips from the film can be used for multiple things. You may want to send it to local news or video outlets when you do an interview so they have b-roll to cut to. You can also use them on social media. Actors will certainly share and repost a scene that they worked so diligently on. It will surely drum up interest if you have some awesome moments that tease the viewer but don't give everything away.

6 PR Strategies

Let's get into the different routes you can take to get coverage and build buzz around your film in post-production. There are all types of PR strategies that you can look up, but I want to give you the outlets that my firm goes after. So bust out a pen and paper because the following are the ways that you will now start to engage the public.

1) Traditional Earned Media

Earned media is that which cannot be bought or owned. So basically, if you aren't getting the attention through economic means (paid media) or a media outlet you have control over (owned media), you have to work to get it. Let's work!

The traditional types of media are radio, TV, and newspaper coverage. This is where that list that you created in pre-production will come in handy. As you reach out to different outlets, recognize that no outlet is the same. A newspaper has a certain amount of space that can be used on a page. A television news program has two to three minutes for a segment. Depending on the radio show, you may have the length of the show to speak or just a smaller segment.

My point is, know the outlet and tailor your messaging to it when you reach out about coming on their show or trying to score an interview. No outlet has time to get your pitch together for you or to try to understand what your film is about. Make sure that everything is clear in your communication the first time because first impressions are everything, and second chances are rare.

How to Conduct Yourself in an Interview

The interview process and how your conduct yourself is so important! Within minutes of my Picture Lock interviews, I can always tell who has experience in interviewing and who doesn't. For me, it just means that I realize I will have to direct the interview in such a way that my questions hit what my guest may not remember to cover, but that doesn't always work for other formats.

If you're doing a three minute segment for news, you don't want to be carried by the host due to your lack of preparation and you can't go back. Watch professional interviews to understand how Hollywood professionals do it. You can find all kinds of examples of red carpet, radio, and even newspaper interviews online. What you'll notice is that from the actors to the directors and everyone in between, they have a stump speech. What I mean by that is that you hear the same responses across multiple interviews with minor adjustments and room for creativity depending on who they're talking to. They can quickly answer what the film is about, who their character is, and the major events that happen, but without giving away any spoilers.

Practice conducting an interview in the mirror or as you sit on the couch. By walking through possible questions of any outlet, you'll start to work out any kinks and get your answers embedded into your brain. This will really help you so that when it's showtime and you need to sell, you can have fun during the interview rather than searching for answers. Preparation will help give you confidence and help you put your best foot forward.

Your interviewer can feel your experience, but more importantly, your potential audience will be listening and feel it, too. Speak to them through the interview and convince them to get behind your film.

2) Speaking Opportunities

Speaking opportunities are a little harder to come by, but if you can land them it is a great way to get noticed. The reason that they are harder to come by is because speaking engagements usually are for an expert or advanced person in whatever space they may be speaking in. On top of that, there are usually a finite amount of speakers at any given event, and events themselves might be hard to come by.

Positioning yourself early in your career as someone who can talk on a specific subject regarding film is key. If you're a recent college grad, you can speak on making the transition from school to the real world. If you've been doing this for years and have numerous features under your belt, you can share your knowledge on finding sustainability within filmmaking. If you're a minority filmmaker you can speak to a specific demographic as well. Embrace your niche, life experiences, specific filmmaking skills, and career stage in an effort to market yourself as a knowledgeable speaker or expert on your subject matter.

This is also where networking usually comes in. Having a great product will definitely get you noticed and can open doors. However, knowing the right people and making yourself known and available to opportunities to speak will help if this is an option you're looking for. It never hurts to ask directly, either. You'd be surprised what doors will open for you when you initiate the interactions!

3) Strategic Partnerships

Many people focus on earned media, because earned media is the "sexy" attention. Who doesn't want to go on TV and share a radio interview with friends? One awesome move that you can make for your film is to find a strategic partner in order to accomplish this.

You form strategic partnerships simply by associating your film with an organization, person, or entity that can mutually benefit from what you're doing. One of the best strategic partnerships I've seen in action recently is Warner Bros partnering with My Gym. I have two kids ages six and four, so my wife and I take them to the local My Gym to play, have fun, and to give us a little break. As soon as you walk up to the store front you notice (or don't notice but it's there and that can work on a sub-conscious level) a large poster for the film *Smallfoot*. Inside, there are *Smallfoot* worksheets that children can take home to play with. I even found myself working on it with my son when we got there early one time.

Seeing this genius use of PR and marketing in the real world at a level that affects me personally, I asked one of the employees about it. He informed me that they implement things in the curriculum at My Gym that correlate to the movie. He also said that the studios give them the marketing materials months in advance. Then, by the time the movie trailers start hitting your TV, let alone come out in theaters, My Gym parents and children already know about the film. At the time of me writing this, *Smallfoot* had been in theaters for a month and the material was still there.

The reason I bring up this example is because this is strategic partnering at the highest level. Warner Brother's *Smallfoot* is an animated movie targeted for young children. My Gym is a worldwide children's fitness center oriented towards young children. By partnering in some fashion, Warner Bros. is reaching its target demographic of young children and parents of young children in one swoop. My Gym is able to create a fun environment and use modern and relevant films to help boost their curriculum. It's a win-win for both parties.

How can you do the same thing with your film? Think about your target audience and then think outside of the box as to who could mutually benefit from aligning with your work. You may not have millions of dollars to put towards posters and worksheets, but you do know how to make a one location shoot to cut down on costs for filming. Think the same way in regard to your marketing materials. Maybe it's one poster in the local coffee shop and a free screening giveaway for their customers to see your documentary, *Where Do Those Coffee Beans Come From?*. It doesn't have to be big or cost an insane amount, but a well-thought out plan will work wonders.

4) Digital Media (podcasts, blogs, vlogs)

When it comes to these types of digital mediums, you can directly reach the demographic that you feel your film will be great for! The best part is that each outlet has their own built-in audience. If you have a film about stay-at-home moms who decide to start a business together, it may be great to find mommy bloggers or a mommy-preneur podcast.

Go back to that list of outlets and add contacts that you think would be a great fit to be interviewed on. Don't just think about yourself, remember your cast and crew. If your cinematography is top notch, perhaps there's a good blog about cinematography that your cinematographer would be great for. You could look into podcasts about acting for your actors to potentially be on. Again, remember to think about this with pinpoint accuracy but also a little looser outside of the box.

You can sign up for free on sites like podcastguests.com and receive a weekly e-mail with a list of podcasts that are looking for guests. The mixture of a variety of podcasters are perfect for you to look for a specific match and try to get on something that may be outside of the box.

5) Social Media

We covered setting up social media in pre-production. In post-production you want to focus on the messaging that you're putting out into the world. Understand each platform and how they can be used for getting attention.

For instance, Twitter is great for conversations. You can start a good dialogue with a specific hashtag that people can find and add to. YouTube is a great platform for creating videos that can be shared, but because it's created by Google it also serves as a way to archive content.

Your film or interviews will hopefully build and snowball over time.

> Reel Thought: *Don't tag organizations or people as a way to syphon their audiences, get likes, or shares. It's not about that. You should make a genuine effort in who you tag or the organization. If it seems self-absorbed, it probably is.*

Remember in Chapter 3 when I was talking about using social media and tagging people or organizations that may be loosely tied to your film? Well let's talk about that now. As an indie filmmaker, in an effort to make as many people aware of your film as possible, make sure you tag people or organizations that may have an interest in your film. I'll talk about how you can get more specific with this during your festival circuit run in a bit, but the concept starts here.

Let's say you have a film that deals with the sexual abuse of a young child, specifically a boy, that promotes awareness and the need to create change. An organization like 1in6 would be perfect to tag in a post. Something as simple as "Our movie wants to raise awareness and create change in the area of sexual abuse and assault against men, something @1in6org fights to do each day! Check them out at 1in6.org #1in6 #yourmoviename".

Remember, if you can form the strategic partnership before posting, that's the best option because you can form a plan for co-promotion. However, as an indie filmmaker, you may not have the relationship and your post may help initiate a strategic partnership, or give a viewer of your film a resource to turn to. I know that was a heavy example, but it's a great example of how you can make your film more than just a film. It can serve as a conversation starter, a resource, and a link to opening doors for your audience. Whether your film's subject is challenging or lighthearted, by making more than the obligatory "check out my film" post you can appeal to new audiences with your film.

6) Film Critic Associations

The major difference between hiring a PR firm and going at it alone is that the firm has a list of critics and contacts from all over the world. You might not have a massive list or the relationships they do, but that can change. One hidden gem that I don't think many filmmakers recognize is that every film critic association has a website. This is huge because you have a centralized location for finding film critics right at your fingertips.

By visiting the websites and finding out who the members of their association are, you will discover accredited critics you can reach out to. At minimum, the site will link to each critic's social media platforms. Some have their website address linked to their name. Follow the rabbit holes and start a spreadsheet that lists which association the critic is part of, their name, e-mail address, and the genre or audience that you think they fit in. The genre portion is very important because most critics review all films, but have a specific audience. Some critics are heavy into the comic world, others may have an African American, LGBTQ, Latinx, Horror, or female-centered audience. As time moves forward you will be able to specifically communicate with critics that your film will be a good match for.

Use this list to contact each critic with an individual, personalized e-mail. You're doing that because a group e-mail is not personal and it's easy to push off or unsubscribe from. As a filmmaker working independently from a PR firm, you want to make sure that your attempt to communicate with that film critic is seen not as random, but as intentional. Addressing the things about their work that you enjoy within the e-mail is often a plus as well.

Reaching out to critics and creating a list is a key step in becoming an army of one! This part of the process is lost on most indie filmmakers, for whatever reason. Don't miss the opportunity to build community with critics.

CHAPTER 6
THE FESTIVAL CIRCUIT

When your film gets accepted into a festival, it gives it credibility. It means that it made it through the ringer of screeners/judges and the festival programmer(s) believe in the film's production quality and story. As a critic and festival director, when I see laurels on a film's poster, I look at what festivals the film has been officially selected for and/or won an award at. If there are mid-major to major festival names, that's a sure-watch. If there are enough laurels, even though they're not well known festivals, I'll check out the film based on the strength of that as well.

As a filmmaker, the film festival circuit brings you exposure to crowds you would not have otherwise played before. It helps you build buzz and validation for your film. They certainly can help open the door to opportunities for networking that you wouldn't have otherwise. Plus, you get feedback from a live audience, even if it's just listening to laughs (or a lack thereof) during a scene that was written to be funny. The experience is worth it.

Since the audience for this book is independent filmmakers, we'll assume that your film won't be going straight to the theaters. Just because its first stop isn't the local AMC is not a bad thing. Most of the Oscar contenders start out at festivals, build a buzz on the circuit, get some critical acclaim, and then after being nominated, make their way into your local theater. This is a part of the game that I've seen from the inside annually as a member of more than one critic body.

The festival circuit is a business in itself. I believe that film festivals are absolutely necessary as a part of the overall industry. Festivals discover new voices, help to tell wonderful stories that may not make it to the big screen otherwise, and they enrich our communities culturally and financially. So, how can you navigate the film festival circuit without breaking the bank? How can you make the most of your time at a festival whether before, during, or after it? I've got some thoughts for you. Keep in mind these tips are geared for a film festival and not a film market festival.

When to submit?

EARLY! You need to submit during the early submission period for a couple of reasons. One, the cost is cheaper. If you have a limited amount of money, then

Reel Thought: *Make sure that your FilmFreeway/Withoutabox (RIP) profile is up to date. There are countless times where filmmakers' e-mail addresses have bounced back, or numbers don't work for festivals. Don't let that happen because we don't have time to chase after you, so we won't. Trust me! Also, READ the submission rules. Asking for a waiver to a free submission festival isn't a good look.*

the money that you do have budgeted for festivals should go to early bird entry fees. The later it gets in the submission period, the more expensive it will cost to submit. One way to be pro-active about this is to list out all the festivals you'd like to get into. Go to their websites after you have your list and find out when their submission dates are. Put those dates on your calendar and set reminders so that you can be sure to submit on time and during the right period.

Second, the films that come in during the early bird period are the films that stick in the programmer's mind. For my festivals, I make sure that everyone who submits has a fair shot at getting in via the judging rubric. The cream of the crop rises, the bad films sink, and the ones in the middle are the tough debates. Even with that, put yourself in the programmer's shoes: If you saw a film in the first couple of weeks of the call for entry period being open and you liked it, you're going to still be thinking about that film once call for entries (CFE) closes. The early bird gets the worm and has a lasting impression.

Hacks & Tips: Fee Waivers, Discounts & Requests

There is one thing that every film festival needs in order to be a film festival. Can you guess what that is? Right- films! Without films to show, there is no film festival. So if every festival needs films and you have one, then there is a major likelihood that there is a film festival out there that your film will be a good fit for. What does this mean? You have a certain amount of power in asking for an entry waiver or discount. You have to be realistic about how good your film is and know simultaneously what level of a festival you may ask for a waiver. If you're a filmmaker who doesn't have big stars or a major producer to your film, getting into Cannes on a waiver may be an extreme request. However, if you define the tier you'll fit into, you can move forward from there.

To understand this, let's define the types of film festivals. Top tier film festivals would be Sundance, Cannes, Toronto, etc. These festivals receive at least five figure submissions each year because they are the creme de la creme. Mid-range film festivals would be Slamdance, and SXSW (which I predict may jump into the higher tier soon). Niche festivals would be those that are specific to a genre, theme, or specific group. Some examples would be the American Black Film Festival, DC Asian Pacific Film Festival, Big Queer Film Festival or Miami Web Fest. Regional festivals are those that are in your area or look for films in their specific area.

Narrow down the film festivals that you believe your film will be a good fit for and then make a plan to approach those festivals to see if you can get a waiver. Be open to options. While you may want an entry waiver, you should be open to a discount if it's offered. Beggars can't be choosers and honestly, the possibility of having your film play at the festival is more important than whether you were able to get into the festival via a free waiver or not.

What should your ask look like?

This is the most important question. There are tons of e-mails that come through the festivals I've directed that ask for waivers. This is something we expect to see as festival directors and staff. There is a way in which you should make your request that many filmmakers aren't aware of. Sometimes the will and desire that causes you to ask, written out in a heartfelt e-mail, can make an impression, but you're not the only one asking. What will separate you from the pack?

I have an example in the Resources section of this book as to what your ask should look like. In short, you want it to catch the reader's eye by inserting a couple of images (likely the movie poster and a still). You should have the summary of the film and any accolades that it has received whether it is official selections in festivals, winner laurels from festivals, or quotes from critics.

Be sure to put a link to your trailer in the e-mail so that if the reader is interested, they can check it out. Again, this is where having a dope trailer is important! You could say "screening links available upon request", or you may want to consider inserting your screening link with password so that the curiosity of seeing the film may entice the festival or critic.

What to do during the submission period.

This next part depends on the festival size and staff, so proceed with wisdom. I've seen certain filmmakers who keep my festival in the loop on how their film is doing by either sending an e-mail update on occasion, or tagging the festival via social media when their film is accepted in another fest or wins an award. It's pretty smart on their part.

It allows the festival to see that other festivals are accepting the film and in some cases, lets my festivals know they have an award-winning film on their hands. Now the reason I said proceed with caution is because this could be a turnoff if you're e-mailing too frequently. However, a friendly e-mail every once in a while doesn't hurt.

Tagging on social media platforms, like Instagram, is a really great way to be unobtrusive while keeping the festival aware of your successes. In fact, I really think it's something you should do at a minimum, especially if you have a decent following. Remember, festivals need to sell tickets and they want to exhibit films that do well with an audience. Do not misconstrue what I'm saying into some idea that festivals can be bought or sell-out to the highest social media following. I'm saying that if your film is one that they select to exhibit, knowing that it is doing well is icing on the cake.

Marketing before, during and after the festival

Let's talk about how you should specifically be marketing before, during and after the film festival that your film is accepted into. First thing, make sure you make an announcement on your film's website and all social media platforms and tag the festival. Exhibiting your film is a collaborative process between you and the festival. We love to see a filmmaker spreading the gospel about their film, excited about being a part of our festival, and helping in the marketing process.

What tends to happen in lower tiered and niche festivals is that the festival wants eyes on all films and filmmakers want to have eyes on their film. I've seen filmmakers bring a small group to their film's showcase and abruptly leave right after the screening. Do your part! Trust me, we're doing ours, from flooding Facebook, Twitter, and Instagram with ads to interviews with newspaper and tv reporters, but sometimes that isn't enough to fill the house. You'd be surprised how much your promotion as a filmmaker can help with festival attendance. Let's talk about what you can do.

Before

Before the festival you definitely want to post about your film's acceptance. This is when you can start to create a story of your journey to the festival that's part of the overall narrative of your film's journey. For instance, a few weeks out you may want to give an update of the film's status or put up a behind-the-scenes still and say, "DC, we look forward to seeing you in August". Your hashtags are crucial here. Tagging the festivals you're accepted into and their cities helps in your exposure. Think outside the box on those tags. Can you add the film office of said city? A local arts organization that aligns with your film? Or if your film is about a kid who trips on a baseball and after wearing a cast for months can suddenly throw a baseball faster than any major leaguer...can you tag some baseball teams, or better yet, a doctor's office that specializes in tendon and ligament reparation?

Thinking outside of the box and tying organizations or people who may be similarly related is a way to possibly bring in a new audience. It may not work, but it's going above and beyond in your efforts and going against the norm that ultimately pays off. This is what a PR firm would do. Who knows, maybe that doctor may want to come on board as a producer. The point is, for the cost of sweat equity, you can make new connections.

Don't wait on the festival start date to start making connections with other filmmakers who will be apart of the festival. You can find out whose films are already accepted, do a little research and reach out via social media. Repost, DM, Retweet, make an early connection so that you can build relationships and your network. By the time you get to the festival you'll be able to have some good coffee talk with your cohort that will last for years to come. Plus, when you support them and their film, they will support you and yours.

Speaking of not waiting for the festival, why wait for critics or the press to know about your film? Find out which critics are in the city your film will be at. Figure out what local film bodies are active there. Who is the arts and entertainment journalist for the local paper? Reach out to those people and invite them to come see your film. Make sure you're not reaching out the day of. Reach out two to three weeks before so that they know you've put some thought into it. It's not going to make an impact if you do it the week of.

This might also be a time where you want to send an e-mail, rather than just tagging someone on social media. Make a more personal connection with them. It shows the person that you took the time to construct a message to them personally, rather than making them an additional person tagged. Again, maybe nothing comes of it, but you might just get that one critic's attention who wasn't planning on seeing your film at the festival, but now they will just because you reached out.

Some festivals may have special workshops for screenwriting, producing, etc. with limited spacing. I can't tell you how helpful it's been for me as a filmmaker to partake in them in the past. Jump on those quickly. The relationships built in those workshops will go far beyond the workshop. Plus, many times it gets you in the room with industry pros who have tons of knowledge to share.

Also, make sure you have postcards, posters and business cards printed in time for the festival. I'll get into the whys in a bit, but in general, you're trying to maximize exposure for your film while displaying professionalism.

Here is one nugget of wisdom that you should hold on to: Make sure that your cast and crew get a lot of love during this entire process! This should start during the casting and pre-production process, but should certainly continue on the festival circuit. You didn't make the film alone! Don't act like you did. Film is a collaborative effort, and the more you can share some shine on your co-collaborators, the more of an army you'll build.

Make sure to tag your actors as you put up the behind the scenes photos and footage you worked so hard to capture in pre-production! One, they love to see the images and footage too. Two, they'll definitely share the images and footage. It's a win-win for everyone involved because the film and the individuals get to show "we were here" and "we made a film".

Finally, do not post your film on the internet before your festival run! This may seem like a no-brainer, but most festivals will not play your film if it can be seen for free online. That doesn't help sell tickets. Also, from a sales perspective, no one will want to license the film either. Again, this is all scalable. If you have a web series, than it being online kind of comes with the territory. You can always reach out to the festival for clarity on their rules.

During

In person and online marketing. Tell the story of what's happening with you during the festival. Document the journey via all social media platforms. Again, try to make sure what you're putting out has your authentic voice and that anything you do put out sheds a positive light on your film.

This is also where having your postcards or a poster to put up where you can will come in handy. You may want to contact the festival ahead of time to make sure that if you brought a poster, you'd have somewhere to put it and they're ok with it. Any way that you can get your film in the mind of patrons coming through is helpful. That way, when they see your film in the program they think or talk about it.

Network. Network. Network. You have to exchange numbers, cards, or whatever you may have during the festival. Hopefully, you've already broken the ice with other filmmakers before the festival. Be sure to follow up with those you've been in contact with. If you get back home after the festival and you feel tired, you probably did your job. With new, meaningful contacts to add to your rolodex, catching up on sleep will be worth it!

Press: Most members of the press receive badges that identify them as just that. Make sure you have a conversation with those folks. Whether you're big time or not, most press in attendance love talking film. For us, it's also a great to get to know the person behind the film. In fact, you'll find that most film critics and film journalists having a genuine conversation with a filmmaker, actor, producer, etc. is welcomed when done the right way. Think about it, we both love film, we just come at it from different angles. That press member will engage if you're up for it.

Keep in mind, most people know when they're being hustled. Filmmakers know when their film gets a lot of love that the press will be anxious to talk, and vice versa.

We, the press, know when someone has an angle. That's kind of difficult because at the end of the day we all have some angle, but again, that's why I say make sure you're genuine.

Remember to play the long game. I'm sure you will be making films for the rest of your life. You don't have to score your first time at bat. Sometimes just getting on base is all you need to do. "Hey, can I come on your radio show and talk about my film?" isn't the best initial point of contact. What if the critic didn't like your film? What if he or she doesn't have time to talk? Feel the situation out and at least introduce yourself and tell the name of your film. You can always follow up with an e-mail later. Some critics attend certain festivals annually and serve as a panel judge.

Build your film's community! A theater full of people just watched your film. If they dug it, I'm sure they'd be willing to hear more about what the film's plans are next. Be sure to build your e-mail list by not just sharing your social media handles during the Q&A, but having a sign-up list ready to go when people approach you to talk about the film. The folks that are interested in talking with you after the lights go up are going to be your zealots. Put in the time with them. Don't leave the room empty-handed. Even adding two more e-mails to your list is better than zero.

After

Post-festival marketing. Make a post about any awards you received or even just the good time you had. Again, be sure to tag the festival, as well as your film cast and crew. Festivals enjoy seeing photos they may not have taken and they like to see filmmakers having a good time. Your continued participation in the marketing process will certainly leave an impression with festival staff.

Provide festival feedback. Leave a review of the festival on the platform you used to submit your application. The festival may also have their own survey to gather information on your experience. Be honest. That information can help improve the festival. I love getting five star reviews on my festivals, but I truly appreciate getting honest feedback even more. Not to say that anyone has been dishonest, but I want my festival to be the best experience for everyone involved. I know I can't achieve perfection, but if there are issues that I can improve, I certainly want to know what they are.

Consider distribution. When is it time to stop promoting your film? Well, your film will likely have a twelve to eighteen month life span on the festival circuit. It works this way because festivals are an annual thing. Sundance kicks things off in January and there are festivals through December. If your film does well on the circuit, you can have a long run in which festivals continue to play your film due to the rack of laurels and awards you've accumulated. The key is to make sure that you've made connections along the way. Right before your festival run is about to dry up and you've made the most of every opportunity, it's time to look into distribution. We'll talk more about distribution in Chapter 7.

Technically, you should already have your distribution idea and plan put together in pre-production, but there has to be flexibility for the unknown. Perhaps you get tapped on the shoulder after a screening of your film at some festival by a manager. Maybe someone wants to buy your film. Planning is great, but be open to change.

Know what's next! Have your next project in the works. There's a few reasons you need to have something ready to go. One, to answer the inevitable question of what's next? You should never be without words for that question. Whether you have a script that you can pitch, or you're already in production on your next film, you should have something to say. It shows that you're serious about your craft.

Two, it gives an opening for possible collaboration. Have you ever wanted to go to lunch with a co-worker? When you come up to their desk and their food is there, well that answers that question. However, if they haven't eaten yet, then you can ask. In the same way, you're at the festival with your lunch at your desk. They get to see your film and think to themselves "they have good taste". So when they're asking if you have something else in the works, it's a possibility to get some lunch with you next time and share in the movie process. That may have been a crazy metaphor, but we all gotta eat!

CHAPTER 7
DISTRIBUTION

What's your goal?

S
ometimes the goal is simply to make back the money you spent making your film. Sometimes it's paying back your investors, or making enough to make the next film. Whatever your goal is in getting your film distributed, it should be clearly defined in your distribution strategy and should fit the scale of your production.

If you want your film to be on Netflix, do you know what the Netflix standards are? Is it a documentary you're hoping to shop to PBS? What are the technical standards? Are there any similar films on whatever platform that you would like to be on? If so, what are the things that may have led them to get a deal? Figure these key things out so that you can go into the distribution process having a film that meets the criteria. That said, you should definitely be thinking about distribution in pre-production.

I truly believe that as long as you have a solid film, especially if it has been selected to show in multiple festivals, there is a platform out there for you to make some money off of distribution. You could turn the film over to an aggregate like Distribber who will distribute your film to iTunes, Amazon, Netflix, Xbox, and more. You could also seek out niche streaming services like

KweliTV that curates films from the African Diaspora. You have to look at what rights you'll be giving up, if any (some entities offer non-exclusives), but do your research and you can find a way to make your film exist and bring you some income, large or small, after its circuit run.

Distribution Strategies

A biblical proverb says that, "Plans fail for lack of counsel, but with many advisers they succeed". I'm not a lawyer, so as you start to get into the nitty gritty of rights and selling your film (if it comes to that) be sure to get legal counsel to protect yourself and the project. Make sure that you hold all the rights, or at least know everyone who holds the rights to your film when it is time to start inking deals. Outside of seeking legal advice and counsel, you should also ask questions of filmmakers who have treaded the water before.

One of the major reasons I wanted to write this book is because I want to make sure indie filmmakers don't allow their films to fall to the wayside due to a lack of vision for its distribution. I hate seeing an amazing film on the festival circuit only to never see or hear about it again. I think this happens because filmmakers aren't prepared for the marathon and it can get tiring after making the film and running the festival circuit. Don't let this be you. Find counsel in filmmakers that have done it before. Even if you have distribution from another film, you can still seek wise, professional advice on your new project to ensure optimal success. Here are some buzz-word strategies.

Video on demand (VOD)- Video on demand is a default for indie filmmakers. It provides instant access to your film at a low cost that's either to rent or to own. The question here is, do you want your film to reach as many people as possible or do you want it on a specific platform? Knowing your film, and your audience will inform your decision.

Self-distribution- It's the old, do-it-yourself, sling it out of your trunk, or sell from your website strategy. The pro here is that there is no middle man. You have a direct transaction with your consumer. The con is that unless you have a huge following, you're going to really have to work hard to be able to bring people to purchase your film.

Limited Release- This is when you release the film in a small number of theaters. Depending on how well the film does, you may pay to have it stay in theaters longer or increase the number of screens and locations it plays for.

Simultaneous Release- A simultaneous release is when a movie is made available on various platforms and in theaters, all at the same time. The pro of a simultaneous release is that you can have one marketing campaign to rule them all. The date doesn't change and it's easy to promote during interviews. The simplicity of a simultaneous release can be helpful for your marketing strategy.

Interview with Filmmaker Devin Gallagher

I've had the pleasure of knowing many filmmakers who have gotten distribution for their films. I wanted to make sure that I got the perspective of filmmakers I know and trust to give some straight talk in my online course, PR For The Indie Filmmaker. The course hits many of the topics we've covered in this book and more. As a living course, it goes into more depth as I continue to add to it. As a part of the distribution section, I sat down with Devin Gallagher, director of *Married in Span-dex* and *Kandahar Journals* (both are documentaries), to talk about the distribution process and what one should think about and expect in seeking and getting distribution. Here's that conversation:

Sampson: Alright, so I'm really excited to be talking with my friend Devin Gallagher, who is the director of *Married in Spandex* and *Kandahar Journals*. Dev, thanks for taking some time to talk with me today.

Gallagher: No problem.

Sampson: So, this is a course in which we're looking at PR for the indie filmmaker. And I think one of the things that I did want to touch on is distribution, you have a lot of experience with that with the films that you've made. And so I just wanted to pick your brain on a few things, and see if you could give some insight to the people that are watching this. So the first question would be, what's the first thing that filmmakers should do, just in terms of thinking about distribution? So, if we could talk from a pre-production, production, post production kind of strategy.

Gallagher: Yeah, I think it's important! One of the most important things is to think about where the film is gonna end up as you're developing it. I think that actually has a lot to do with how the film is going to look and feel. And I think, for example, if you're seeking funding through PBS, or public broadcasting, nine times out of ten, they're going to become a partner in the film, if you're applying for that type of grant funding. If you are looking to get on Netflix or Hulu, the standards are really tight. So that's something to keep in mind, in terms of where your dream is at, and maybe thinking about the reality of what is possible.

Also in terms of the channels and the platforms that you are looking at, they have specific branding and specific audiences that may have really specific needs in terms of content.

Sampson: So, what I'm gathering from you, you're saying that, basically, when you're approaching pre-production think about where you specifically want your film to be. So I could have a documentary and it's geared maybe for more the PBS type market. Go ahead and start thinking about that, and looking at what are their standards for distribution on their platform, as well as, like, if you have, let's say, a horror film that you think might be great for Netflix, just looking at what those standards are? Is that correct?

Gallagher: Yeah, that's the technical specifications, as well as the kind of more qualitative, thematic, or content that that may be similar to what you're trying to produce and what they've recently purchased.

Sampson: Okay, so with what you just said, if x footage can't be on Netflix, that would mean that in pre-production, you have to figure out what camera to actually use? Is that what you're saying?

Gallagher: Yeah, and it depends. A lot of times, it's a certain amount of footage, particularly for documentary because there is a lot of legacy footage that you collect or archival footage that you collect. So it depends. Sometimes they have different ratios. So you really have to check it, and it's on their website. So there's no mystery. It says exactly what they accept. I'm sure if you create, you know, the best documentary of the year, and it happens to not be shot on Alexa, they're still going to go after it. But the standards are there for a reason, so that people know going into it that if the target is Netflix, you really want to be putting the budget together that supports the equipment that you need.

Sampson: Let's move into production. What are some of the things that you should be thinking about distribution-wise, or maybe setting up? Are we talking to or making phone calls with Netflix or Hulu? I'm sure you can't make a direct phone call with Netflix. But, you know, what should you be doing while you're in production in regard to distribution?

Gallagher: I think it's important to really think of the film that you're making as a small business that you're launching. And so in terms of that, you don't make a product and then go find who might want to buy the product. If you're launching a start up, if you're launching anything, throughout the process you're really trying to develop where this product is going to end up, who's going to be the consumers of the product, etc. And so throughout pre-production/production, you're reaching out to people and giving them little bits of information, maybe pieces of footage, or little trailers to help stoke the flame of interest in your film for whoever is the intended audience for it.

So I think that there's not something that you're actively kind of pursuing. But you're trying to open doors to either more grant funding, or some sort of buzz that can happen around your film so people start talking about it. That way it doesn't just come out of nowhere whenever you release it for the first time.

Sampson: Right. That's one of the things that I've been teaching in terms of making sure that you're building that buzz. You're getting those laurels on the festival circuit, and then trying to do media outreach to have those interviews and things like that surrounding your film. And so I think that what you just said is a really key point in terms of having the distributors are already interested because of the work that you've done with your PR and your marketing so that they see, "hey, this is actually something that is wanted or desired by an audience". Audiences are enjoying this film and want to see that film. So I guess this is kind of a question/statement in that by helping to kind of build that buzz and show that this film is desired or being talked about that can only help in the distribution phase.

Gallagher: Right, and it's not only that, but I think another key component, or a way that people start taking notice of a film is the cast and crew. If you have, you know, like a well-known actor, or a well-known director, or even an editor that people follow. So, for example, what is your editor working on right now? If they get noticed by the industry professionals, then you're more likely to have your film noticed, and have them take a serious look at it.

Sampson: So let's talk about your films and your experience with distribution. So, you have *Married In Spandex*, which is your first documentary feature, and then *Kandahar Journals*. So *Married in Spandex*, if you could tell the audience where you guys landed with distribution, video on demand, and then we'll go into the what that process was like.

Gallagher: So *Married In Spandex* was a shoestring budget of about $15-20K total. We did a Kickstarter, and it was more about a lot of people's in-kind contributions. And my wife and I, Allison Kole, produced it and co-directed it. We billed it as we were first time filmmakers, because there's a lot of you can get away with. Which was true, we were for first time filmmakers, but you can get away with a little bit more of the technical aspects of it because of budgetary issues and other things. But there was some interesting energy behind it, because it captured kind of a subculture.

It was about a lesbian couple that was being married by a lady rapper who wears spandex in Ames, Iowa. Which at the time was the third state to legalize gay marriage. Now, it's kind of become part of the history of the movement. But it was a big deal that Iowa was a place where people from West Philadelphia, which is pretty progressive area, traveled there to be married. The whole, kind of road-trip aspect of it, and the popularity of the actual rapper that married them was significant, so we tried to capture all that.

The challenge became, it was a weird time. So time, in terms of the length of the film, it was an hour long. So that was kind of a weird spot to be in because it's not a short that you can easily put into a lot of festivals and get a lot of attention that way. It was a little bit not long enough to be a feature. So you kind of get stuck a little bit. We talked to several different distributors and it was really interesting. The thing that I remember the most about all of that is, you know, you're kind of bright eyed and bushy tailed because this is your first film and you put a lot of time and blood, sweat and tears into it. However, you have to know that your films, not the next winner at the Sundance Film Festival. And that's the thing that a lot of industry, people try to make sure that you don't have these unrealistic standards of where you think the film is going to end up.

A lot of people thought, you know, their film is going to be in Walmart, and sold around the world. Maybe it's maybe it's a great film, but it's not for everyone, particularly like our film was not for everyone. When you talk to them, you have to understand that. I don't know if it's some of the people in LA that we talked to, I don't know if they're jaded from the industry or what. It's also a sales tactic, I believe, to kind of disparage the film and say something like "yeah, you know, I don't really see a market for this but I'm willing to give it a chance." And in saying that, that is them trying to be like, "well, this guy's about to give me a chance. I have a shot now." You know? When in reality the game is that they, in some cases, try and get as many films as possible. They sign these deals, where they get a bunch of films and if one film takes off, then they make their money.

In our case, because we were so close to the story and so close to the film, I'm not interested in someone representing my film that doesn't even think it has a market or says that out loud to me. So that was, that was kind of an interesting situation where we were just like, "No we're not interested in working with you." But beyond that, you keep trying and keep talking to people. Eventually, you find somebody. The person that we went with was snag films, which is a great distributor. They focus a lot on documentary and they have a mantra that documentary is "filmanthropy", they call it. So it's about, giving these stories for the social good, as opposed to maybe a money making venture. It was a great time to get in with them, because they were really excited about the film. They actually said, "we love your film", which is a big deal. After having all of those other meetings with other people.

Then from there, it took a while. It does take a long time to get the film processed. Because depending on who you go with, sometimes they have a big backlog. They have to go through all the processing of the material and get the trailer and poster and all that together. Then we ended up finally getting distribution on Amazon, on Snag films website itself. Then on Hulu, as well.

So, we were featured on Hulu. Mainly it was just web distribution. So we did our initial festival tour, which is more about kind of getting them out there and in front of audiences. For us, it wasn't about necessarily selling the film from the festivals but you have to go through that process to say to the distributor, it's been seen by ten thousand people, or a couple thousand people, here's the reaction, here's the news, here's the buzz around it. Then they make an assessment based on that.

Sampson: Awesome. So, that goes straight into what I've been talking about in regard to building your buzz. Having your film's journey be told as you're going through the festival circuit and even in the production process is important so that once you get to the table to talk distribution, you have that paper trail. You'll have those numbers to be able to present to the distributor.

One of the things that you mentioned, which I think was good is the expectations of knowing whether your film is top notch, high quality, or this is a great film but it probably isn't going to make it to a nationwide theatrical release. Knowing that, but then also knowing your film's value. So, looking for a distributor that is as passionate about your film as you are, I think that's a really important point. It seems as though you had multiple meetings with different distributors, which is probably helpful, because that way you've spoken to a variety of organizations so you get those contacts in your Rolodex. Also, it's almost like finding your wife in that you date other people. So you're like, "Okay, when The One comes in, you're like, yes, this is the one!"

So, switching from *Married In Spandex* to *Kandahar Journals*, which was a little bit larger in terms of distribution, because you guys had distribution in Canada, if you could just explain a little bit about the film and how distribution worked with that film.

Gallagher: Yeah, so Kandahar Journals is a documentary about a photographer who spent several years in Kandahar, Afghanistan as an independent journalist. We took his thousands of still images and eighty hours of footage and told his story. It was kind of the war presented through his eyes and it focused on the psychological transformation that he went through throughout the years of covering war.

For something like that, we definitely did experience the initial, you know, if you say, "Well, I'm working on a film about Afghanistan", people go, "Oh, that's interesting". You get that initial hit of interest. It isn't something that would end up on History Channel, or anything like that, instead it ended up being more of an art film. It had very little dialogue, very little talking head and was more of an experiential film. So because of that, that kind of left us with only a narrow opportunity for distribution. But part of the interest and part of what made it special was it was a Canadian film. So in Canada, Canada had a huge involvement in the war in Afghanistan, particularly in Kandahar. And for the Canadian audience, it meant a lot to have this kind of historical document. I think, is why we had a lot of success distributing in Canada specifically.

So from there, we were on the CDC, Canadian Broadcasting. We got some national broadcasts of the film on the CDC, as well as its kind of documentary channel. It's kind of like their equivalent of the Sundance documentary channel. And so that played for about two years on that, as well as their on demand platform. So that was a big deal and they came in with a chunk of money to finish the film plus a little bit on the back end. So they kind of took it the last quarter of funding that we needed to get the film done. And so from there, what's nice about that is the film is finished in a format that you can then go and sell to other markets, other countries internationally. We couldn't sell it in Canada anymore because we just did that. A part of the scheme is that you either sell broad rights to a big distributor in Europe, if you're savvy enough, you can pick off individual countries. If it's of interest to kind of the whole world, you can go to every distributor in each country in the world and create your own little deal that that is very specific. So there's good and bad with either of those. We ended up going with a Spanish distribution company in Spain that helped translate it to Spanish, as well as get it into a couple different markets, including South America. Then a German company that translated German. Then they came in with some funds as well.

There's a lot of business stuff that has to happen. A lot of lawyers that have to go over the contracts and different things. So to be able to make those higher level deals, you really need a lawyer to kind of go through that. So there's complexity and all that but the bottom line is getting your film out there. There's a thousand different ways that you can do it, because you can sell off broadcast rights, you can sell web rights. Copyright is a very powerful tool and it's great to have as, as a creator, as a filmmaker.

Sampson: So I am first time filmmaker and at least in terms of seeking distribution what you just said sounds awesome. Like, "Wow, that would be so great. They got the CBC to come in and give some finishing funds. Oh man to go to Spain and get a distributor! But then he's talked about lawyers and all that kind of stuff. That's kind of daunting." So if you could kind of just break down what are those steps? What do I need to do in order to see these deals come together? Do I need to call up an entertainment lawyer, or see who's in my area? And then on top of that, it seemed as though the CBC was already aware of your film. So how did you get them aware of the film and all that kind of stuff?

Gallagher: Yeah, I think that mainly was my film partner, Louis Palou, who is actually the photographer featured in the film. His excellent work of just working the film in every way possible. I mean, he had a long career [and is] pretty well known in the Toronto circles, as well as Canadian circles. So he had access to certain people that were able to help us. But also, there was the Hot Docs pitch. So, there's this whole program for pitching that he went to and he just almost didn't sleep that whole weekend. He just talked to every single person that was there, really just selling the film. This is something, in terms of your team, if you don't have someone like that on your team, it's a huge disadvantage. If you can get someone that has the confidence and just the tenacity to go out and even if someone's not interested, they're going to hear about it, you know.? I think that makes a huge difference in the back end of when you're going to sell the film and having multiple people interested. And then you end up with maybe one or two that you go with.

Sampson: Alright. So again, that kind of goes into the whole marketing and networking while you're at these different festivals. And the importance of why you should go and why you should be sure that you're making those connections. But if you could, just talk about how you have this connection, you have your film, what's the next step in terms of do I need to bring a lawyer in? Then on top of that, how do I make the phone call? Do I need to go to Hulu.com and find a number for distribution? What are those steps to take to get to actually sitting down and talking with a distributor?

Gallagher: Yeah, I think there's two routes. This gets into a little bit of the hybrid model or self-distribution, because there are a lot more opportunities for self-distribution or as they call it, a hybrid model, where you're selling off some rights to some people, but you're maintaining a certain amount for yourself to kind of work your own angles. But I think if you have a film that really has a lot of buzz and it's doing really well at the festivals, what will happen is you'll find some sort of sales agent. A sales agent will represent you at a certain percentage, depending – I'm not sure what the industry standard is – they'll go to all the distributors and make the deals. Then they'll come back to you with the deals.

Then from there, usually what happens is, whatever the deal is, hopefully there's some upfront money so that then you can pay the lawyers and the lawyers will come after that and say, "Okay, let me do all this work for you." And then you subtract all of that work out from whatever you're making from the deals and then that's what you're kind of left with. Usually it's some sort of 70/30 split or 60/40 split in the actual distribution deal that you make. Meaning they have certain costs that they have to accrue and then after they get that money back you split out at some percentage that you can negotiate, depending on how much they want your film. And that's goes back to the sales agent. That sales agent does that work for you, really sells your film, and really knows the market that you don't necessarily work in every day.

But yeah, that's the traditional model of how it works. And then, hopefully, your film does really well and you get a ton of back end sales and make a lot of money.

(Laughter)

Sampson: Yeah so if I heard you right, you have to get a sales agent. Is that is that accurate?

Gallagher: Yeah. Because that's the thing with the big channels like Hulu, all those channels, and even HBO, if you go on their website they have the same thing where it says they don't take unsolicited submissions. And that means that they don't talk to anybody but sales agents, they only talk to sales agents. So, if you have an uncle that is best friends with a programmer at HBO, that's a different story.

Sampson: Right.

Gallagher: But that's the main way in which they do go about it. For the most part, the reason they don't take them is because they may be working on a very similar project that you pitch them and there's a lot of copyright infringement issues if they go forward and release it after they've accepted your submission. So, there could be legal issues that you sue them for with copyright. So they're very careful about that.

Sampson: Okay. And the reason that I'm asking you these questions and drilling it down is just for the people that are reading this so that they will have those next steps and takeaways as to what to do. So to get a sales agent is this is as simple as looking up on Google "film sales agent" and then going from there?

Gallagher: Yeah, and they're at the bigger festivals as well. Of course, because that's where they're finding films. The big festivals like Hot Docs or Tribeca or any of those festivals that have big companies that are trying to buy things they'll be there. And if they like your film, they'll approach you as well.

Sampson: Gotcha. So that's good to know. Definitely one of those things where, again, being prepared, having your cards ready is key. And there is such thing as a film market festival versus a film festival. So if you're able to get into one of those market festivals, then that's definitely going to be a huge key. So I guess kind of wrapping out here Dev, what's the big advice you would give for a filmmaker, that's just kind of getting their feet wet in distribution waters?

Gallagher: I think the big thing would be some sort of partnership. There's a lot of organizations out there that are not necessarily going to give you a check for $100,000 to finish your film or to distribute your film. But there are a lot of options out there, particularly for documentary or distribution through educational distribution.

The other resource is something like Impact Partners, if you've heard of them. They are kind of a shadowy organization.

(Laughter)

Gallagher: Mail them with your project and what it is and they can connect you with crazy resources, mainly people, that are real players that can come and be an advisor in your film and just push it way further than you could do on your own. I think that gets to a point of the film distribution game has been done several times, and there's no reason that you have to do it all over again by yourself. So finding a project advisor or a filmmaker, that has gone through this process and can guide you and meet for coffee once a month and push you that much further is really beneficial. We had several advisors on both projects, and it's really essential to making the connections and making it happen.

Sampson: Well Devin, I appreciate you giving me your time today, and the nuggets of wisdom that you've given in terms of distribution. Really appreciate it. Thanks, man.

Gallagher: Sure, no problem man.

FINAL THOUGHTS

Remember to think of your film as a small business startup. You're launching a small business every time you make a film. With that said, there's nothing new under the sun. Be sure to get advice and help from people who have done it before. Seek out wisdom from those who've successfully passed through the industry.

We live in a time in which you can get all kinds of free information on the internet and via podcasts. If your podcast subscriptions are only to film podcasts, I'd suggest subbing entrepreneurial podcasts because they deal with marketing issues and community building as well. The knowledge is out there and you get what you pay for. So don't be afraid to invest in yourself financially. If you find a program, advisor, or publicist that fits your needs, take a bet on yourself.

Be sure to let me know how this book has helped you by reaching out to me online or via social media. Tell a friend in film if this helped you. It's my hope that this book has equipped you with information you didn't know or hadn't thought about. I'm looking forward to seeing your film on the big screen! Until then, don't let this be the end of your quest to make it. You're almost there! Keep pushing and you'll break through, even as an army of one!

RESOURCES

Picture Lock Links:

Take my PR For The Indie Filmmaker online course here: https://indiefilmpr.thinkific.com/

Get a partner as passionate as you in your film or film event's publicity: www.picturelockpr.com

Subscribe to this podcast in iTunes to hear interviews with indie filmmakers and solutions to PR & Marketing in the After Show: https://itunes.apple.com/us/podcast/kevin-sampsons-picture-lock/id639359584?mt=2

Be sure to visit www.picturelockshow.com for movie reviews, to find information on how to come on the show to promote your work, and everything Picture Lock!

Find Freelancers:

https://www.fiverr.com/
https://www.upwork.com/

DIY Websites:

https://www.squarespace.com

https://www.strikingly.com

https://www.wix.com/

https://wordpress.com/

Create Your Social Media Army:

https://ifttt.com/

https://buffer.com/

https://hootsuite.com/

Film Festival Waiver and Discount Request Examples

(INSERT YOUR FILM'S POSTER OR AN AWE-SOME STILL HERE)

Dear INSERT FESTIVAL NAME Staff,

(If you know the name of the person of the other side, or are addressing someone specifically, use their name.)

Picture Lock PR (<<<link to your production site) has a new narrative/documentary/(insert your genre here) film that would be a great fit for your festival. Army of One premiered in May of 2019 at the Chicago International Film Festival. Since then, it has played at the Virginia Film Festival, Sarasota Film Festival, DC shorts, and in July of 2019 it screened at the American Classics Film Festival, where it won the Audience Award, Nashville Film Festival where it won the Jury Award for Best Short Film, and other festivals across the country. (List the festivals you've gotten in to, awards received, or notable people in the film that may be eye candy for the reader who is thinking, "Blah blah blah" as they read through. If they're reading, that's a good sign, so wow them but don't be too verbose.)

As a low budget indie film, we've run out of our film festival submission funds, but we would love to play your festival. Would it be possible to help us out with a fee waiver for submission? I've included a link to the film and short description below. Thanks for your time.

Best,

Your Name

Title, Film

TITLE: Army Of One

TRAILER: Insert Direct Link

Link To The Full Movie: www.picturelockpr.com

PASSWORD: yourcrushingthegame

YEAR: 2019

RUNTIME: 95 min

GENRE: Documentary

LANGUAGES: English / Spanish

SUBTITLES: English, Spanish

SYNOPSIS: In the heart of every indie filmmaker is the desire to tell a story. You're Indie Film chronicles the struggle, and the struggle is real!

LINK TO SOCIAL MEDIA: @picturelockshow

Example If You Have a Local Tie In To The Festival

(INSERT YOUR FILM'S POSTER OR AN AWE-SOME STILL HERE)

Dear INSERT FESTIVAL NAME Staff,

(If you know the name of the person of the other side, or are addressing someone specifically, use their name.)

Hello! I was wondering if you are open to accepting waivers? I am an original Washingtonian (establishing the city of the festival) born and raised in the Shaw (establishing being a true local by naming a community) area and now based in Miami. My family has restaurants that have been in the area since the 1980's and we have a lot of support in the area at home with great connections with an audience buzz requesting showings at home; this could possibly be a win-win for both of us. We've been in 25 festivals to date and have not had a Washington DC premiere yet. Either way thanks in advance.

Sincerely,

YOUR NAME

The Short Film pilot teaser follows 45 yr. old Douglas Masterson (Mark Powers) as he tries to save his nephew from a trafficking ring. The deeper he goes, the more he wonders if he'll ever get out.

INSERT YOUR FILM stars Mark Powers as the lead "Douglas Masterson" and is known for CSI, The Flash, NAME DROP, NAME DROP, NAME DROP.

INSERT YOUR FILM also features actor Melony Blackwell of the GREAT DEBATERS (BIG NAME FILM), NAME DROP, NAME DROP, NAME DROP.

'Your Indie Film' - Full-length film

Link: Insert Direct Link

rt:18:25

Password: #supportindiefilm

Social Media Handles: @picturelockshow

www.ingramcontent.com/pod-product-compliance
Lightning Source LLC
Chambersburg PA
CBHW070045210526
45170CB00012B/594